What Does It Do and How Does It Work?

POWER SHOVEL, DUMP TRUCK, AND OTHER HEAVY MACHINES

by RUSSELL HOBAN

HARPER & ROW, PUBLISHERS, NEW YORK, EVANSTON, AND LONDON

WHAT DOES IT DO AND HOW DOES IT WORK?
Copyright © 1959 by Russell C. Hoban
Printed in the United States of America
All rights in this book are reserved.
Library of Congress catalog card number: 59-8970

For
Phoebe, Abrom, and Esmé

... And there is no trade
or employment
but the young man following it
may become a hero ...

WALT WHITMAN

CONTENTS

The author thanks the following manu-
facturers for reference material and advice
which assisted him in making this book:

CATERPILLAR TRACTOR COMPANY
CLARK EQUIPMENT COMPANY
EUCLID DIVISION OF GENERAL MOTORS
NORTHWEST ENGINEERING COMPANY

This is a power shovel.

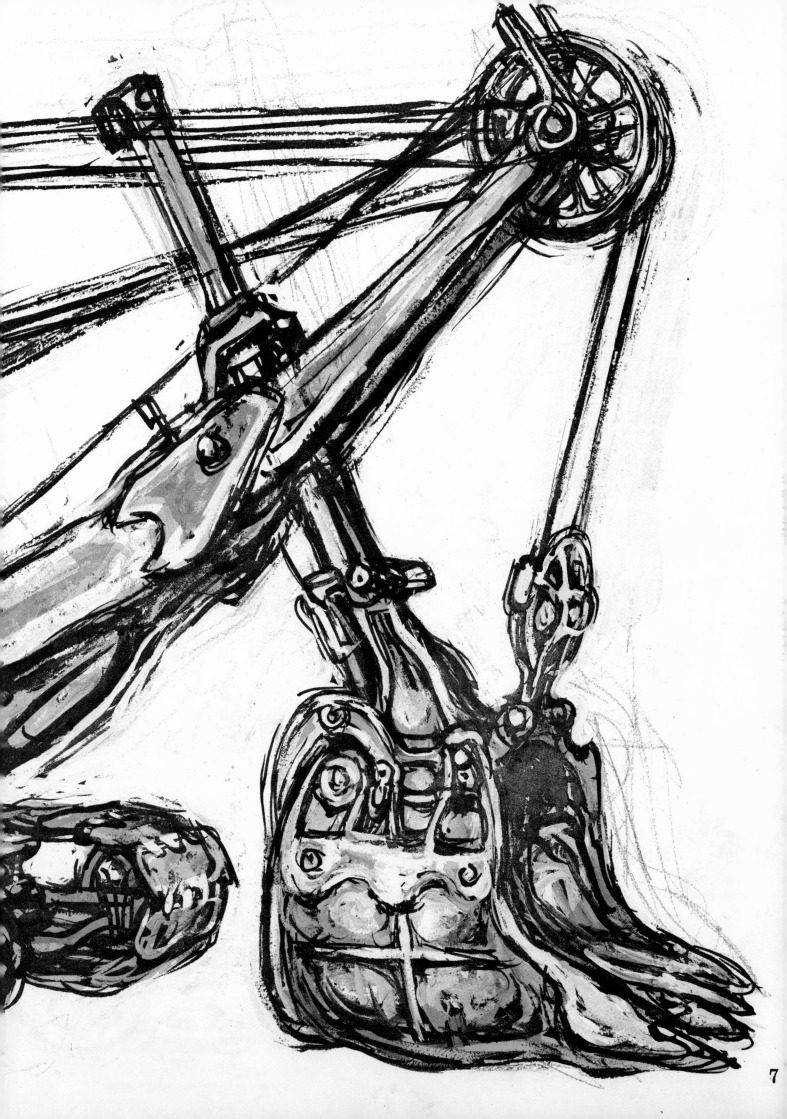

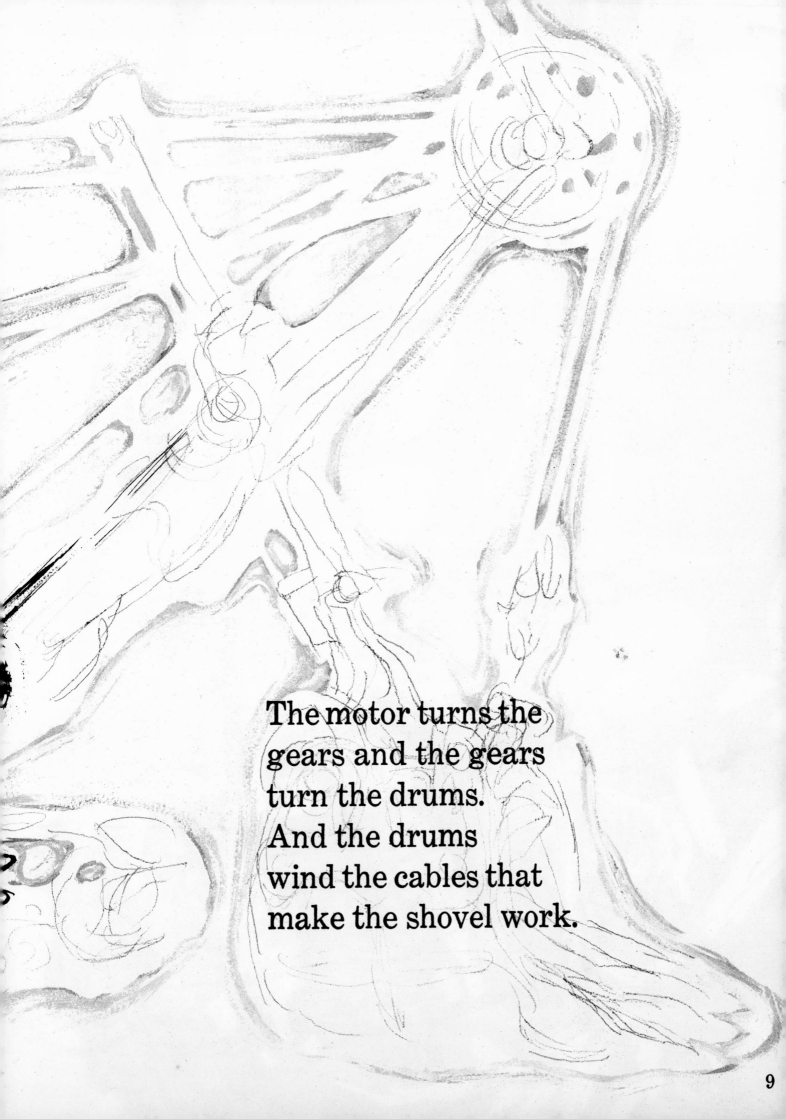

The motor turns the
gears and the gears
turn the drums.
And the drums
wind the cables that
make the shovel work.

Here is where you sit.
And here are the levers
and the pedals that
swing the cab around and
make the dipper
go back and forth
and up and down.
There is a throttle to work
the motor,
a handle to open the dipper,
and a button to blow the horn.

11

The main drum winds
up the cable that
lifts the dipper
with its heavy load
of rock.

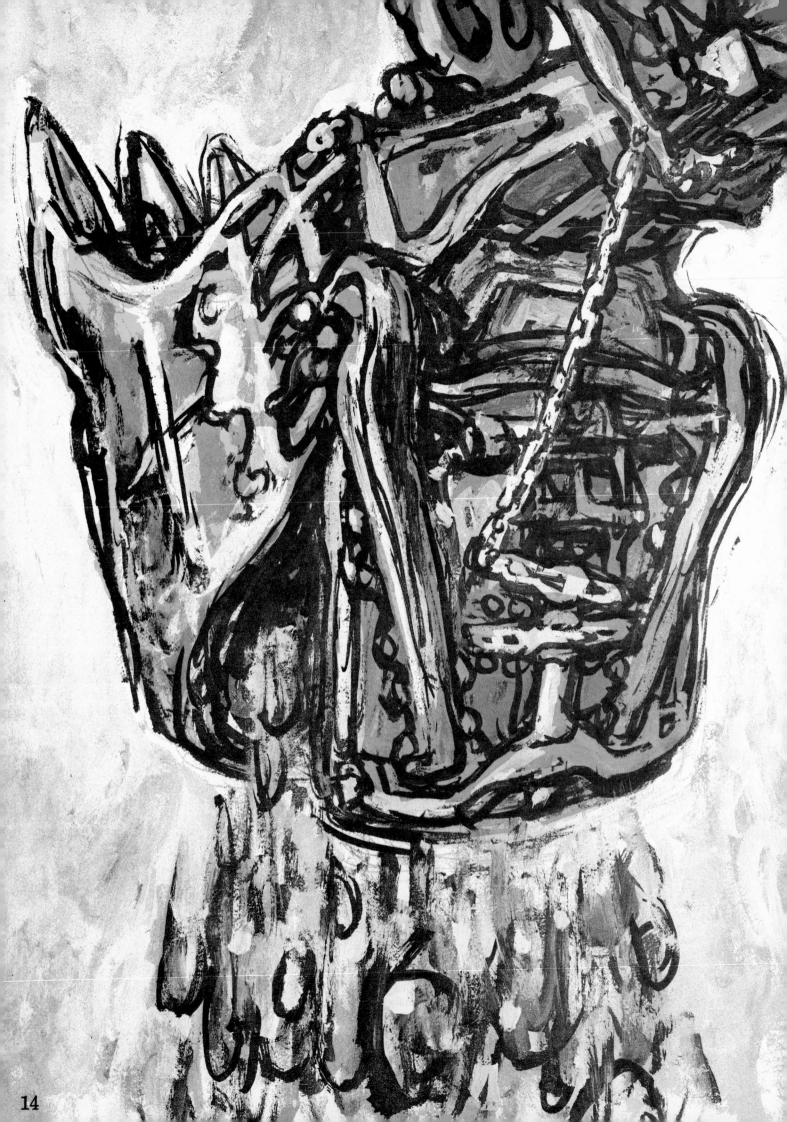

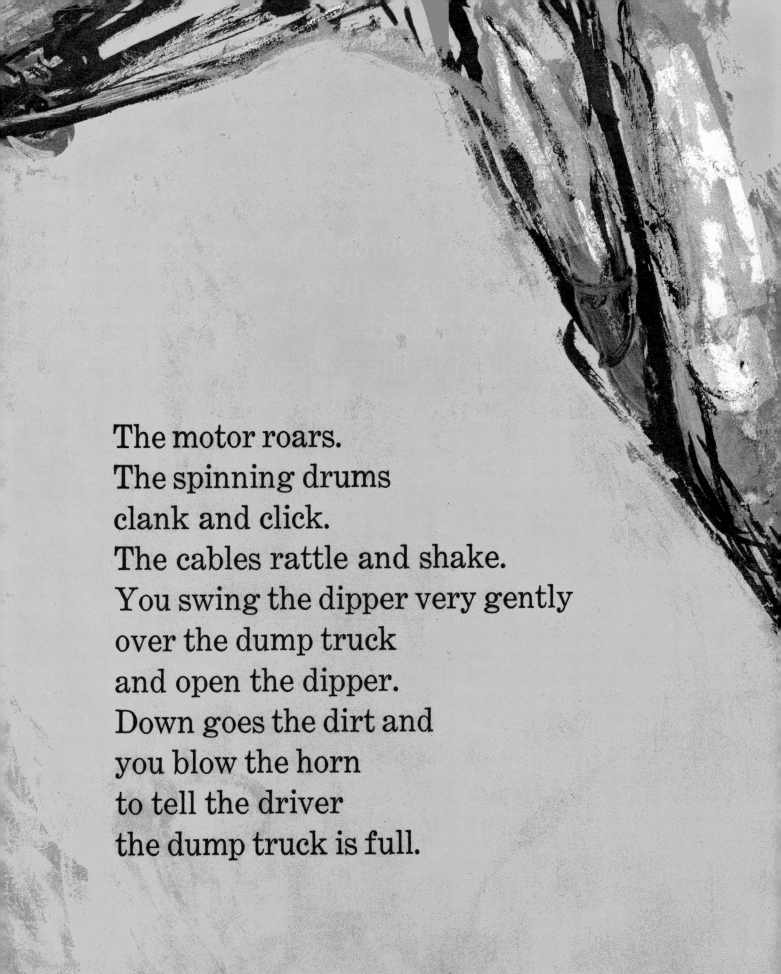

The motor roars.
The spinning drums
clank and click.
The cables rattle and shake.
You swing the dipper very gently
over the dump truck
and open the dipper.
Down goes the dirt and
you blow the horn
to tell the driver
the dump truck is full.

Then back swings the boom
and the dipper digs in—
digging the dirt
and digging the rocks
to fill up the trucks again.

This is a dump truck.

The Diesel engine in
front makes the truck go.
The hydraulic hoist in
back raises the
body to dump the load.

Here is where you sit.
Here is the steering wheel,
and the starter button
to start the truck,
the clutch and the gearshift
for shifting gears,
the accelerator
to speed up the engine,
the brake to stop the truck,
the hydraulic-control lever
to work the hoist,
and a button
to blow the horn.

When you want to dump the load,
you shift the lever
to raise the body.
The pump pushes oil
through the lines to the hoist,
and the hoist opens up
like a telescope
and pushes the body
and lifts it up
so the dirt
and the rocks will slide out.

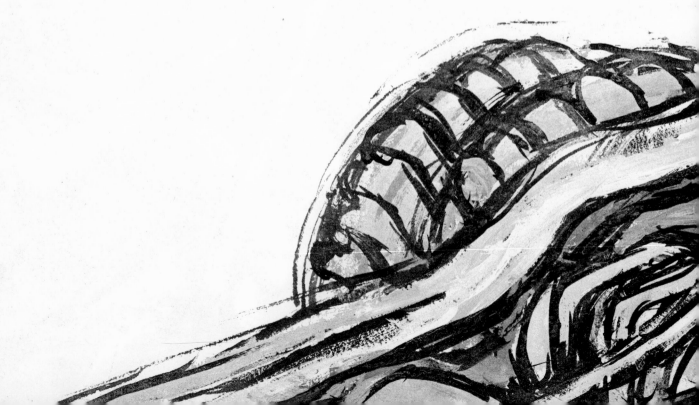

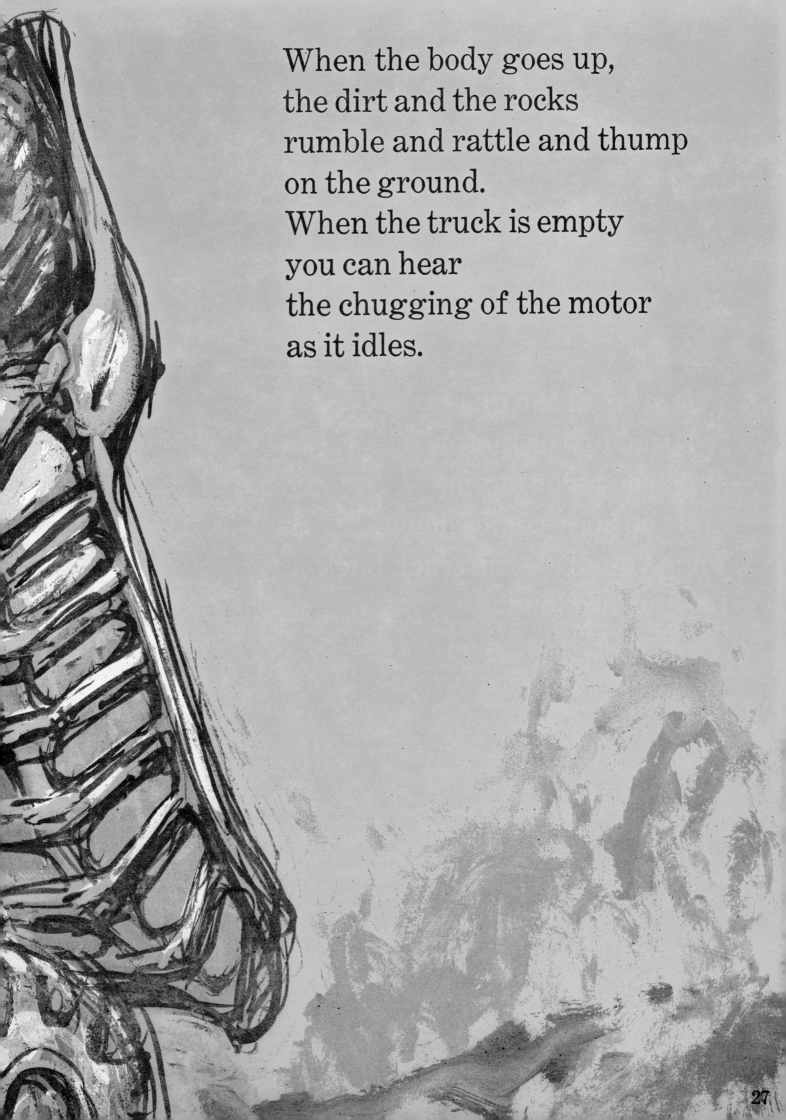

When the body goes up,
the dirt and the rocks
rumble and rattle and thump
on the ground.
When the truck is empty
you can hear
the chugging of the motor
as it idles.

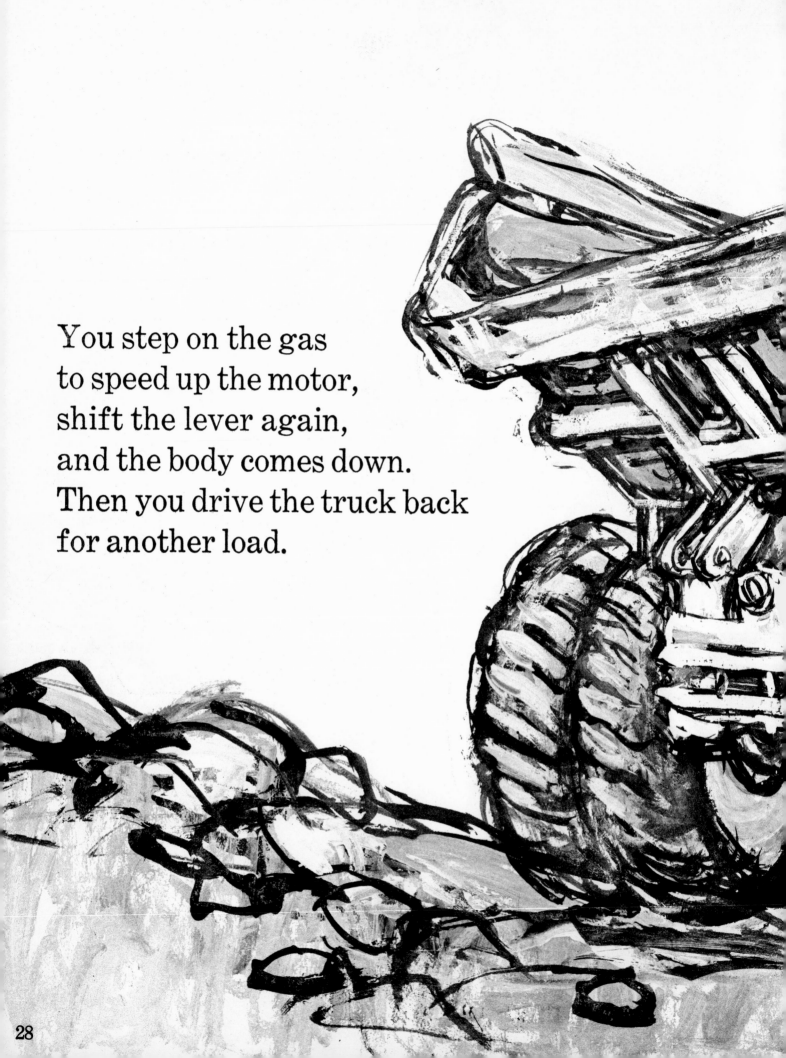

You step on the gas
to speed up the motor,
shift the lever again,
and the body comes down.
Then you drive the truck back
for another load.

This is a bulldozer.

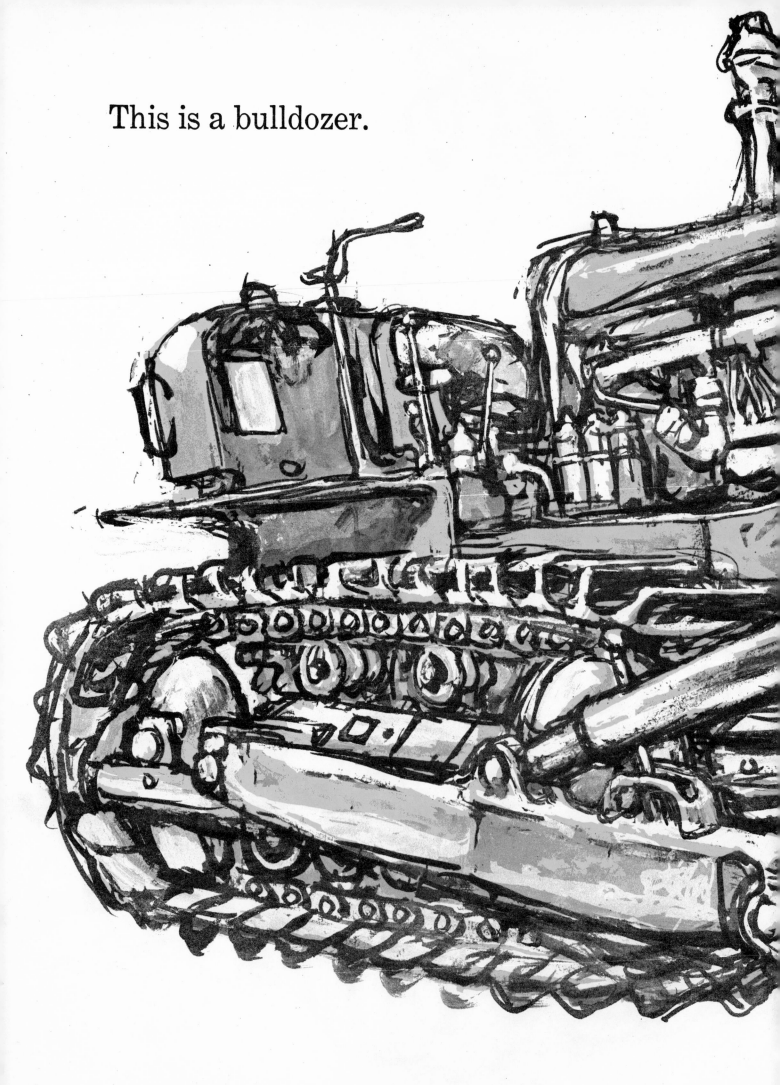

The engine turns the gears
that turn the sprockets
that make the tracks go round.
The cable drum winds the cables
through the sheaves
to move the blade
which pushes the dirt.

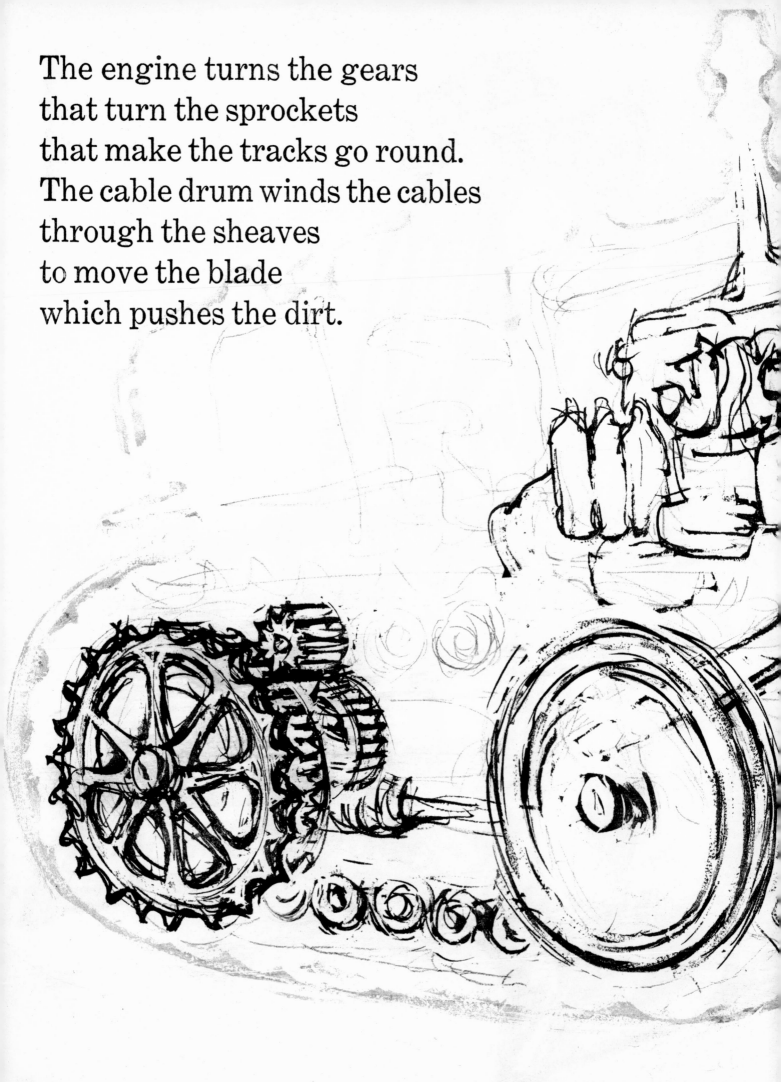

Here is where you sit.
There are two steering levers
and two brake pedals,
one pair for each track.
You steer by stopping one of the tracks
while the other track
swings the bulldozer around.
There is a clutch
and a gearshift for shifting gears,
and a hand throttle
for the Diesel engine,
and a control lever
to work the dozer blade.

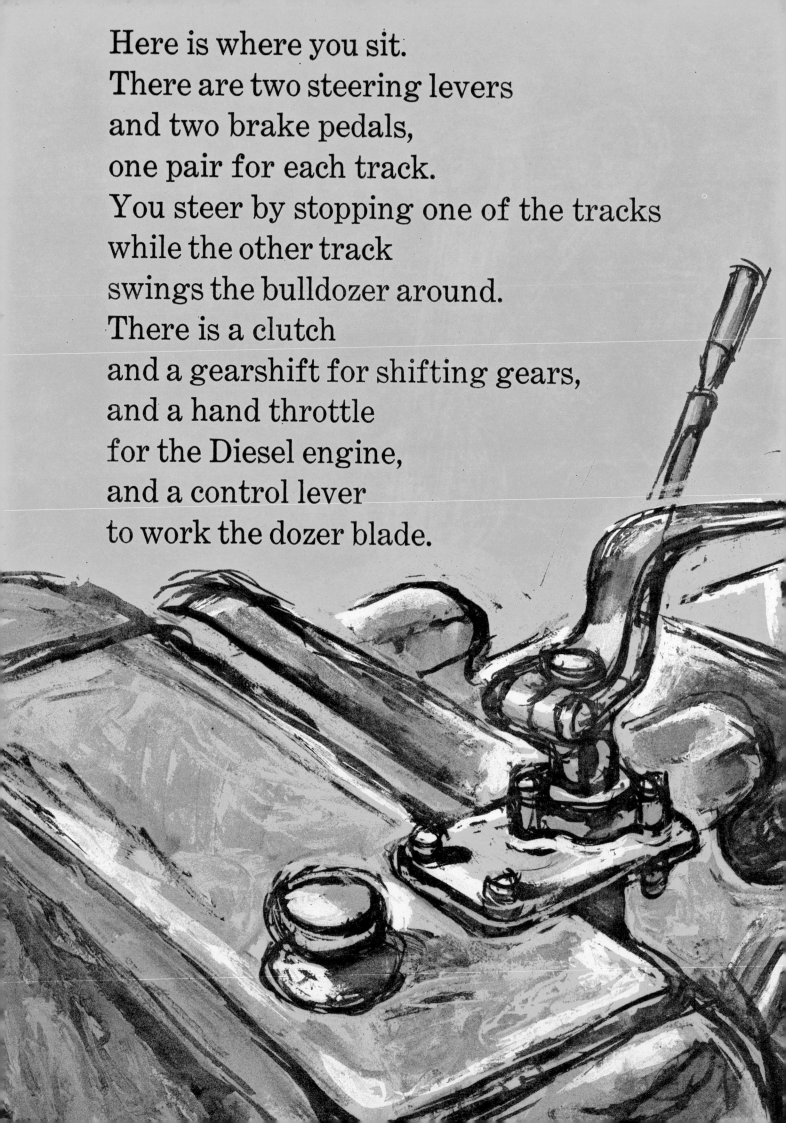

You push the lever
to lower the blade,
and the cable unwinds around the drum,
and the blade comes down
to the ground
to dig and push the dirt.

The blade goes up,
and the bulldozer pushes
very gently against the tree.
You back up, as the tree sways,
then you push again
and the engine roars
as you open the throttle.
The bulldozer quivers and shakes
as it pushes
and the roots tear out
with a ripping sound
and the tree falls over.

Then you lower the blade again
and clear the roots away.

This is a tractor shovel.

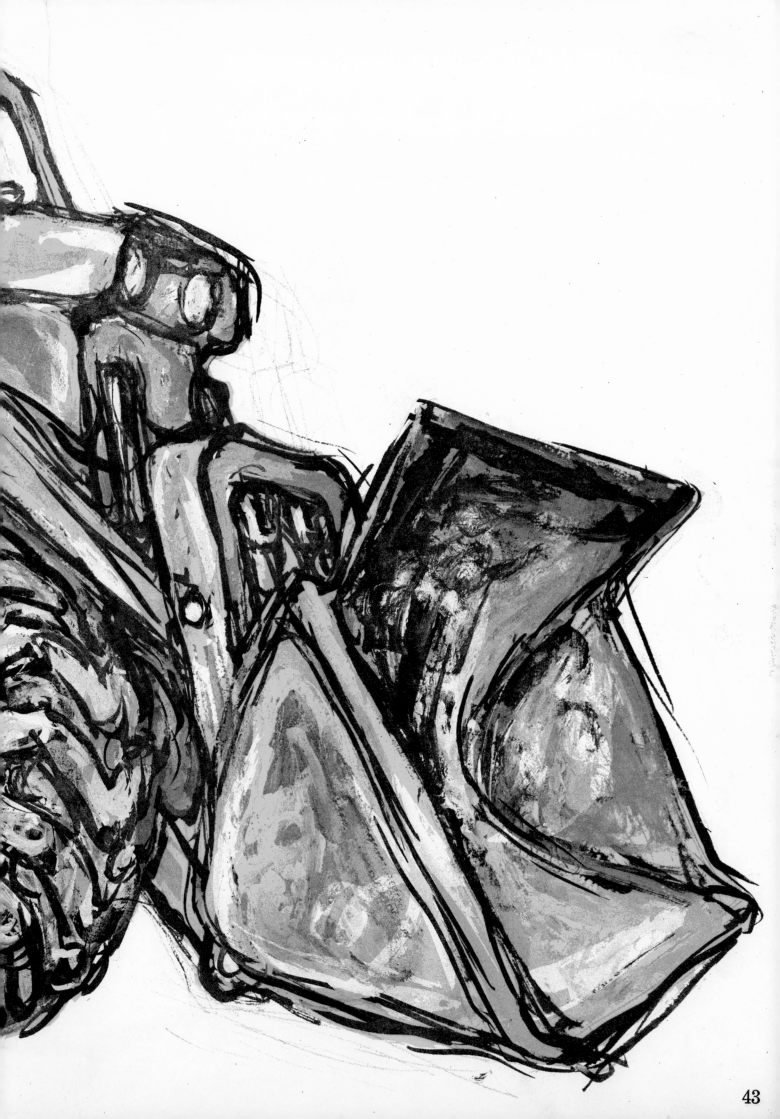

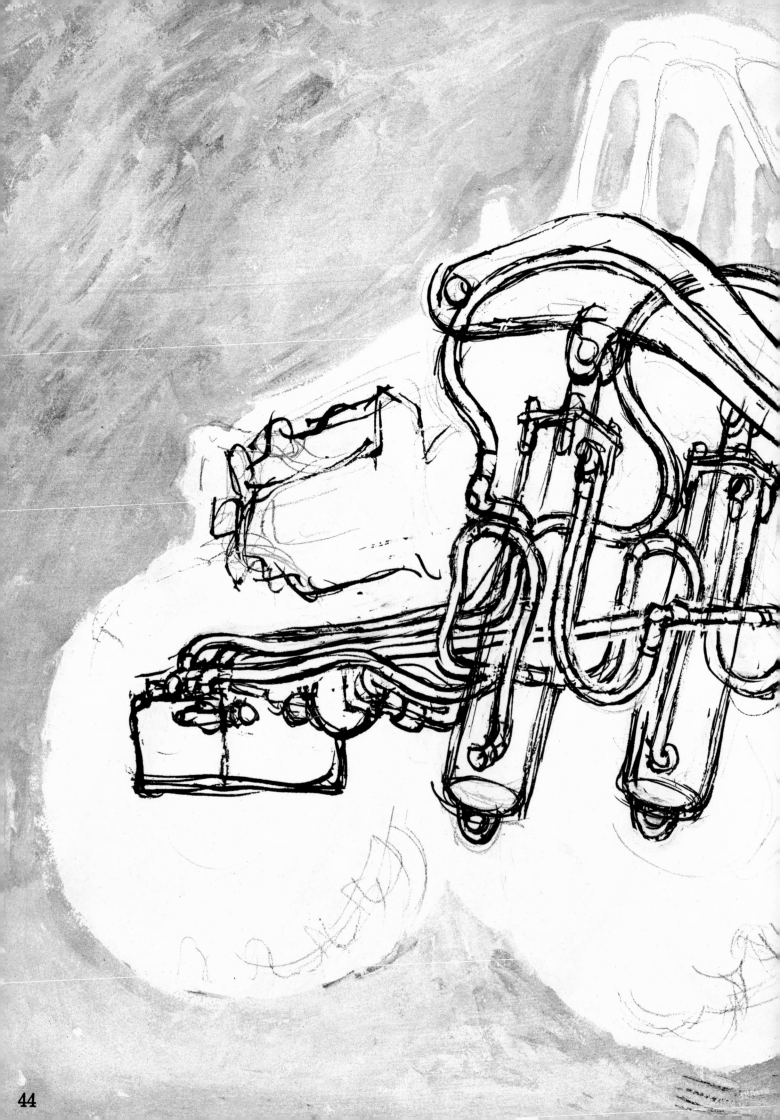

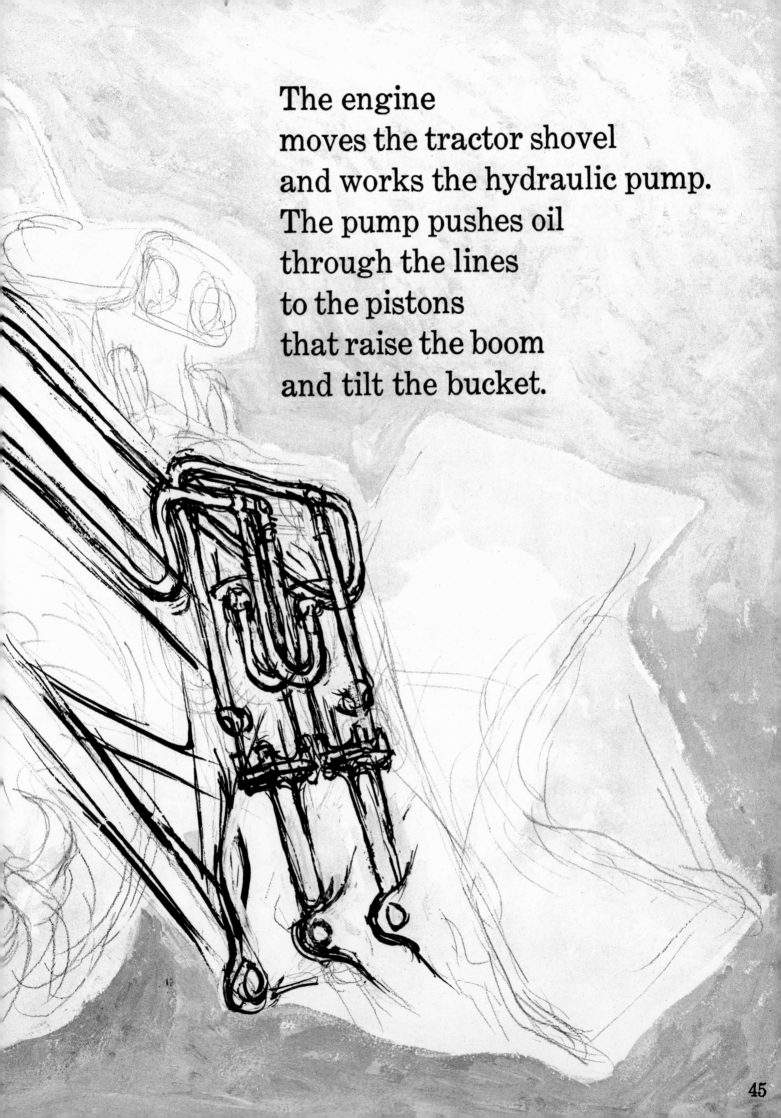

The engine
moves the tractor shovel
and works the hydraulic pump.
The pump pushes oil
through the lines
to the pistons
that raise the boom
and tilt the bucket.

Here is where you sit.
Here is the steering wheel,
and three gear levers
for the automatic shift,
and a lever for two- or four-wheel drive,
and a starter button to start the motor,
an accelerator to make it go,
two brake pedals to make it stop,
a boom-control lever,
a bucket-control lever,
and a button to blow the horn.

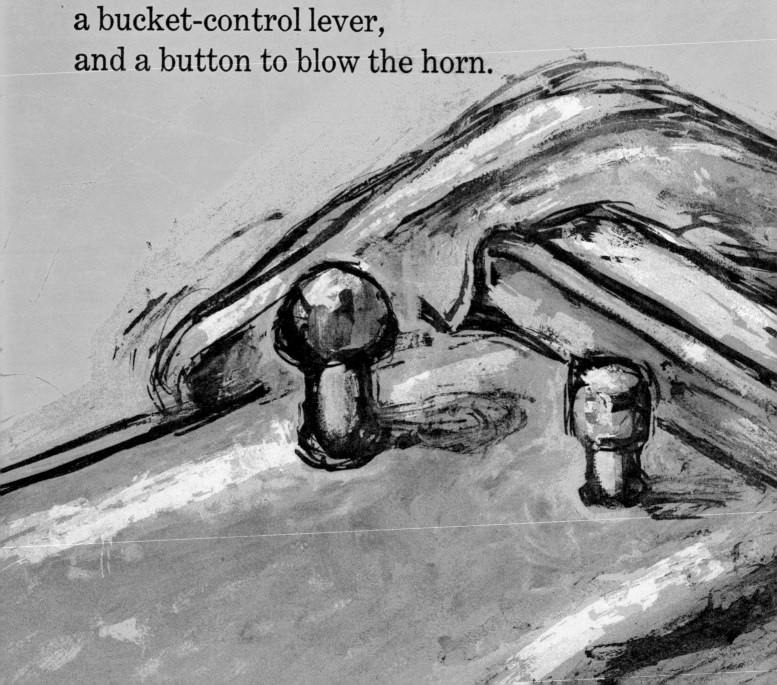

When you pull the boom lever,
the hydraulic pump
pushes oil through the cylinders
to raise the pistons.
The pistons raise the boom
and the loaded bucket.

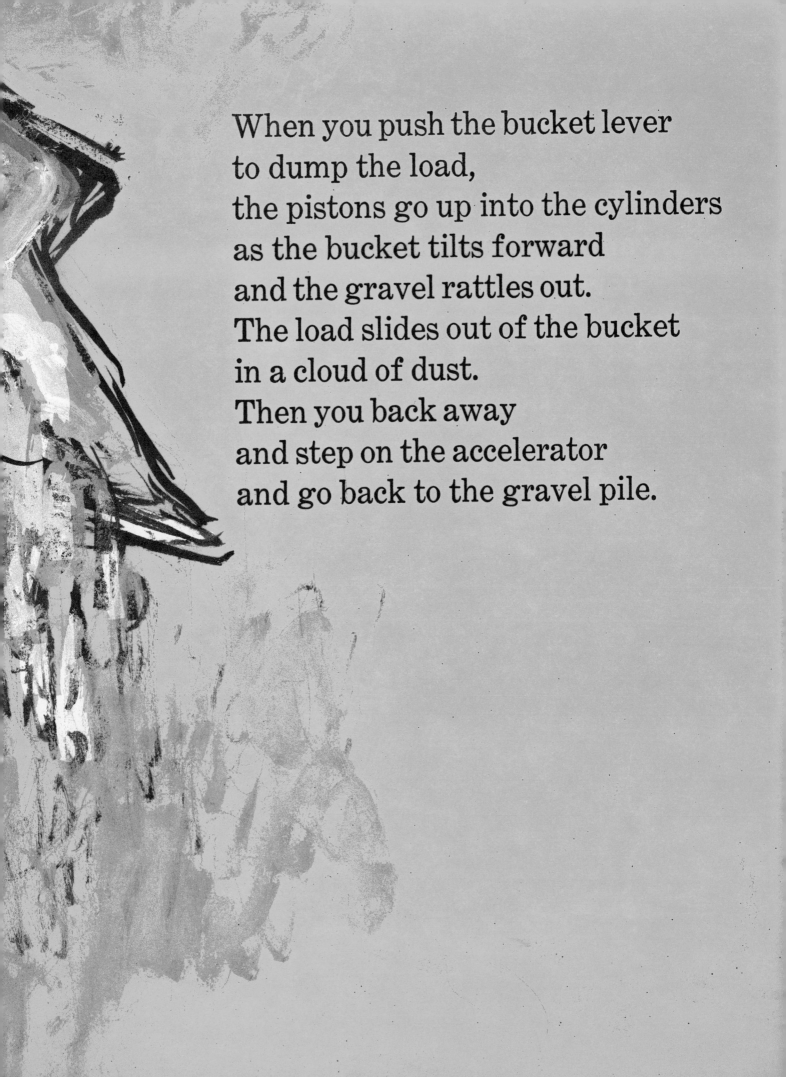

When you push the bucket lever
to dump the load,
the pistons go up into the cylinders
as the bucket tilts forward
and the gravel rattles out.
The load slides out of the bucket
in a cloud of dust.
Then you back away
and step on the accelerator
and go back to the gravel pile.

You lower the bucket,
and scoop up the gravel
for another load.

This is a motor scraper.

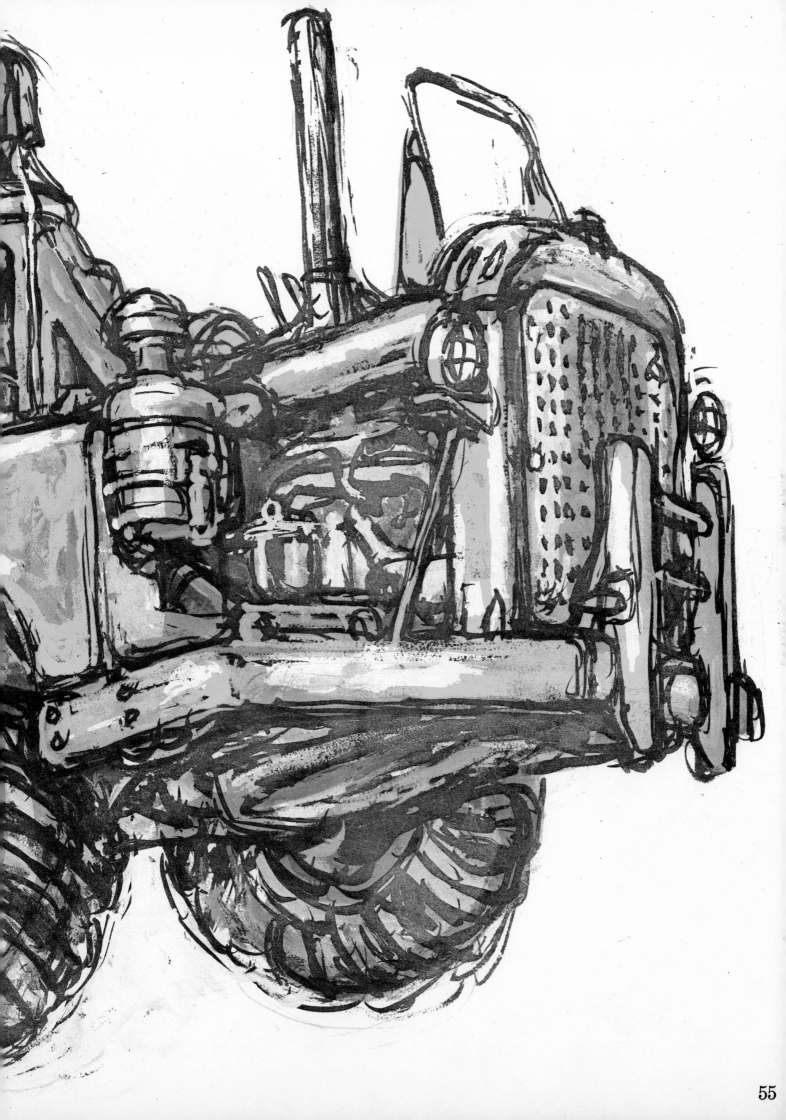

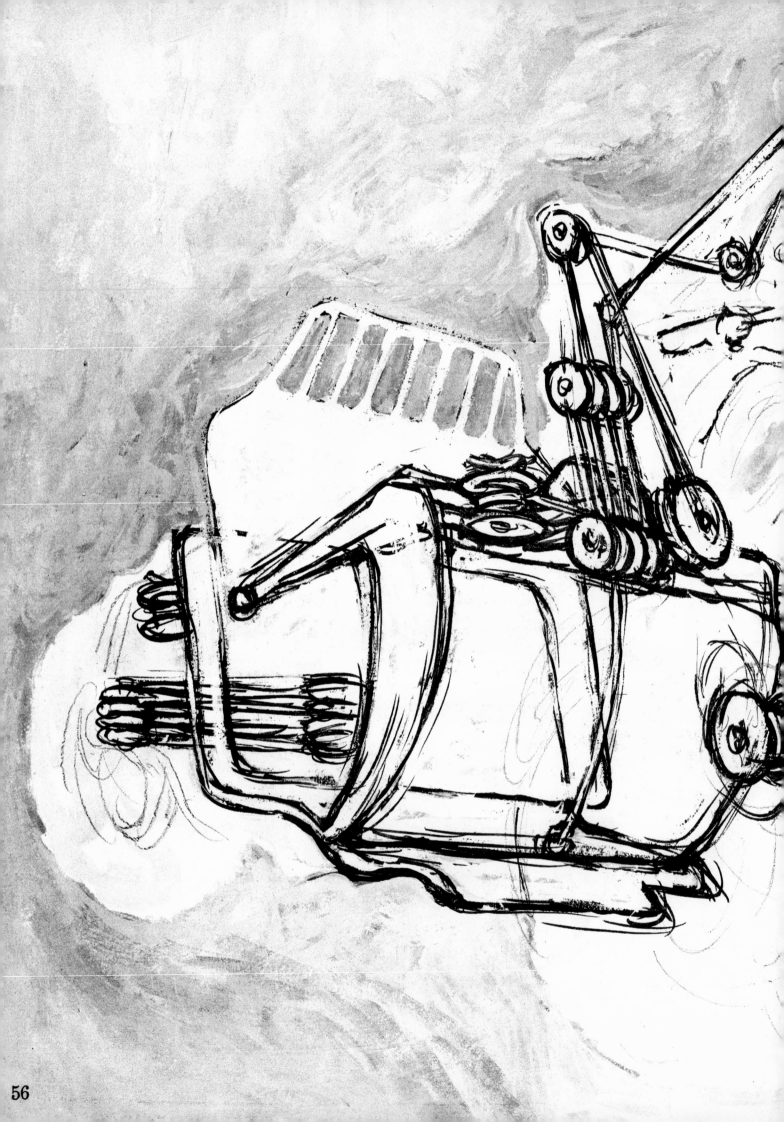

The two-wheel tractor pulls the scraper.
The cable drums and cables
work the bowl
that does the scraping.
The cables also work the apron
that holds the dirt in the bowl
and the ejector that pushes it out
when you dump it.

Here is where you sit.
Here is the steering wheel.
There is a starter button
to start the motor,
an accelerator pedal to make it go,
and a clutch pedal
and gear levers for shifting gears.
Each wheel has its own brake lever
and pedal for sharp turns and stopping.
There is a control lever for the bowl,
a control lever for the apron and ejector,
and a button to blow the horn.

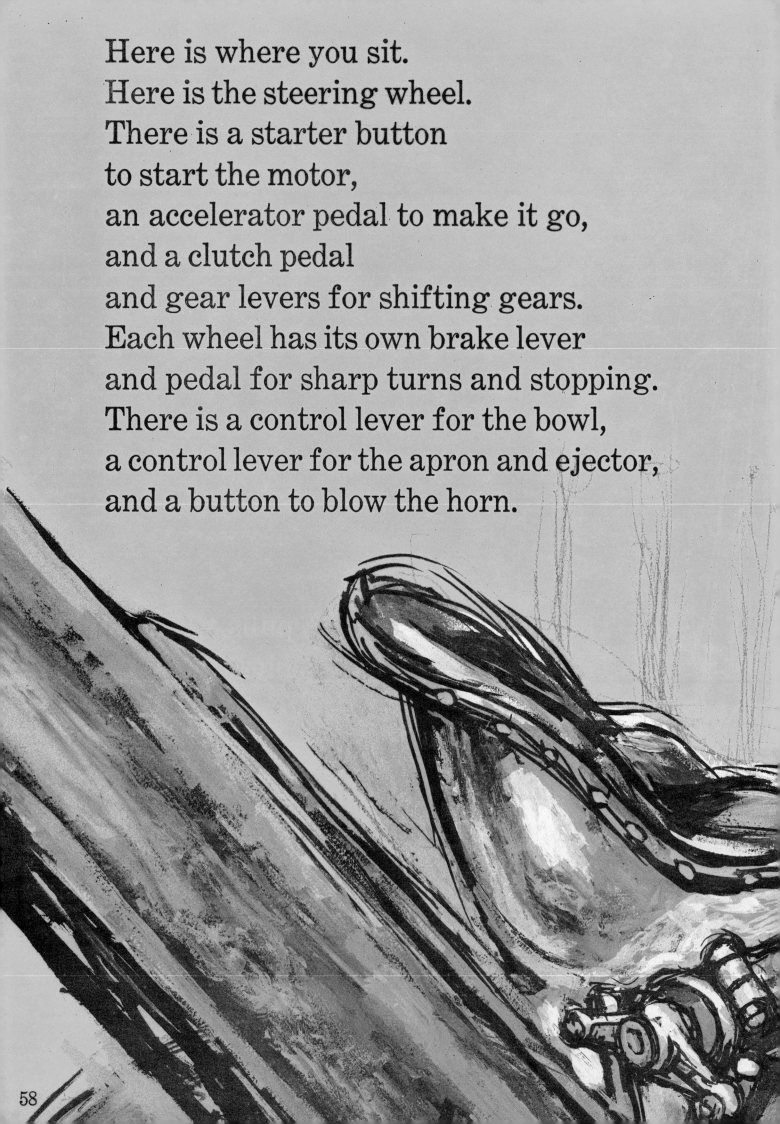

As you lower the bowl with its cutting edge,
the ejector is out of the way and the apron is up
so the bowl can fill up with dirt.
The dirt is heavy,
and a bulldozer gives you an extra push
to load the scraper full.
The rumbling, clanking scraper fills,
and when it is full,
you lower the apron
to close up the bowl,
raise the bowl off the ground,
and haul the load away.

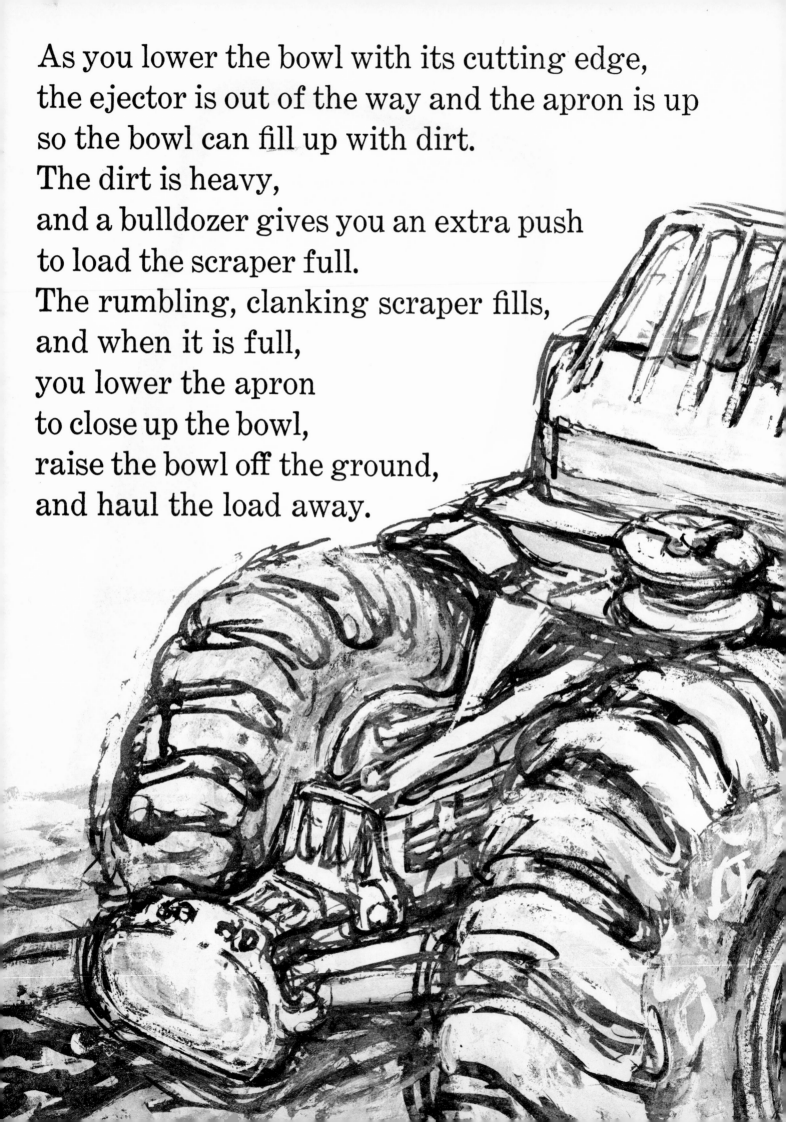

When you want to unload,
you raise the apron
and move the ejector forward
and spread the dirt evenly.
When the bowl is empty,
you go back for more.

E   1

Hoban
What does it do and how
does it work?

E   1

Hoban
What does it do and how
does it work?

P5.5

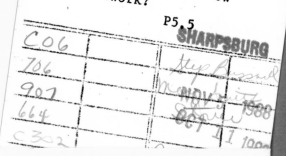